Congressional
Research Service
Informing the legislative debate since 1914 _____

Appropriations and Fund Transfers in the Affordable Care Act (ACA)

C. Stephen Redhead
Specialist in Health Policy

August 1, 2014

Congressional Research Service

7-5700

www.crs.gov

R41301

Summary

Implementation of the Patient Protection and Affordable Care Act (Affordable Care Act, or ACA) is having a significant impact on federal mandatory—also known as direct—spending. Most of the projected spending under the law is for expanding health insurance coverage. This spending includes premium tax credits and other subsidies for individuals and families that purchase private insurance coverage through the health insurance exchanges established under the ACA, as well as enhanced federal funding to expand state Medicaid programs and tax credits for small employers.

In addition, the ACA included numerous appropriations that are providing billions of dollars in mandatory funds to support new and existing grant programs and other activities. Other ACA provisions require the Secretary of Health and Human Services (HHS) to transfer amounts from the Medicare Part A and Part B trust funds for specified purposes. The law appropriated significant amounts to support short-term health care programs for targeted groups prior to the health insurance exchanges becoming operational in 2014. It also created a Center for Medicare and Medicaid Innovation (CMMI) within the Centers for Medicare and Medicaid Services (CMS) and appropriated $10 billion for the FY2011-FY2019 period—and $10 billion for each subsequent 10-year period—for CMMI to test and implement innovative payment and service delivery models.

The ACA established four special funds and appropriated substantial amounts to each one. First, the Community Health Center Fund, to which the ACA appropriated a total of $11 billion in annual appropriations over the five-year period FY2011-FY2015, is helping support the federal health centers program and the National Health Service Corps. Second, the Prevention and Public Health Fund, for which the ACA provided a permanent annual appropriation, is intended to support prevention, wellness, and other public health-related programs authorized under the Public Health Service Act. Third, the Patient-Centered Outcomes Research Trust Fund is supporting comparative effectiveness research through FY2019 with a mix of annual appropriations, fees assessed on private health insurance, and Medicare trust fund transfers. Finally, the Health Insurance Reform Implementation Fund, to which the ACA appropriated $1 billion, is helping cover the administrative costs of implementing the law. Overall, the ACA included more than $100 billion in appropriations over the 10-year period FY2010-FY2019, including $40 billion to provide funding for the State Children's Health Insurance Program for FY2014 and FY2015.

Federal outlays on insurance expansion coverage under the ACA, which constitutes most of the law's mandatory spending, are almost entirely exempt from sequestration. However, the mandatory appropriations in the ACA are, in general, fully sequestrable at the percentage rate applicable to nonexempt nondefense mandatory spending.

Besides the mandatory appropriations discussed in this report, the ACA also is having an effect on federal discretionary spending, which is controlled by the annual appropriations acts. A companion report, CRS Report R41390, *Discretionary Spending Under the Affordable Care Act (ACA)*, discusses the law's impact on discretionary spending.

Contents

Tables

Appendixes

Contacts

Introduction

Implementation of the Patient Protection and Affordable Care Act (Affordable Care Act, or ACA)[1] is having a significant impact on federal mandatory—also known as direct—spending.[2] Most of the projected spending under the law is for expanding health insurance coverage. This spending includes premium tax credits and other subsidies for individuals and families that purchase private insurance coverage through the health insurance exchanges established under the ACA, as well as enhanced federal funding to expand state Medicaid programs and tax credits for small employers.[3]

The Congressional Budget Office (CBO) and the Joint Committee on Taxation (JCT) estimate that the gross costs for insurance coverage expansion will total $1,839 billion over the 10-year period FY2015-FY2024. CBO and the JCT project that those costs will be offset by revenues from the ACA's new taxes and fees, and by savings from the law's changes to the Medicare program that are designed to slow the rate of growth of Medicare payments to certain health care providers.[4]

The ACA also included numerous appropriations that are providing billions of dollars in mandatory funds to support new and existing grant programs and other activities. Several other provisions in the law require the Secretary of Health and Human Services (HHS) to transfer amounts from the Medicare Part A and Part B trust funds for specified purposes.

This report summarizes all the mandatory appropriations and Medicare trust fund transfers in the ACA and provides details on the status of obligation of these funds. The information is presented in two tables. The report also includes a brief discussion of the impact that sequestration is having on ACA mandatory spending. This report is periodically revised and updated to reflect important legislative and other developments.

Besides its impact on mandatory spending, the ACA also is having an effect on federal discretionary spending, which is controlled by the annual appropriations acts. Discretionary spending under the ACA falls into two broad categories. First, there are the amounts provided in

---

[1] The ACA was signed into law on March 23, 2010 (P.L. 111-148, 124 Stat. 119). A week later, on March 30, 2010, the President signed the Health Care and Education Reconciliation Act (HCERA; P.L. 111-152, 124 Stat. 1029), which amended numerous health care and revenue provisions in the ACA and added multiple new stand-alone provisions. Congress and the President have since enacted several other bills that have made targeted changes to specific ACA provisions. All references to the ACA in this report refer collectively to the law as amended and to other related HCERA provisions.

[2] Mandatory, or direct, spending generally refers to outlays from budget authority (i.e., the authority to incur financial obligations that result in government expenditures such as paying salaries, purchasing services, or awarding grants) that is provided in authorizing laws, as opposed to annual appropriations acts. Mandatory spending includes spending on entitlement programs (e.g., Medicare, Social Security).

[3] While a detailed examination of the ACA is beyond the scope of this report, numerous CRS products that provide more in-depth information on the many new programs and activities authorized and funded by the law are available at http://www.crs.loc.gov (see under "Issues Before Congress: Health").

[4] CBO, *Updated Estimates of the Effects of the Insurance Coverage Provisions of the Affordable Care Act, April 2014*, http://www.cbo.gov/sites/default/files/cbofiles/attachments/45231-ACA_Estimates.pdf. For more information on the ACA's projected impact on federal direct spending and revenues, see CRS Report R42051, *Budget Control Act: Potential Impact of Sequestration on Health Reform Spending*, by C. Stephen Redhead.

---

appropriations acts for specific grant and other programs pursuant to explicit authorizations of appropriations in the ACA. Second, there are the costs incurred by federal agencies to administer and enforce the health insurance reforms and other core requirements of the law. A companion CRS report discusses the ACA's impact on discretionary spending.[5]

ACA Appropriations and Fund Transfers

Table 1 summarizes all the ACA provisions that include an appropriation of funds or a transfer of amounts from the Medicare trust funds. The provisions are grouped under the following headings: (1) Private Health Insurance; (2) Medicaid and the State Children's Health Insurance Program (CHIP); (3) Medicare; (4) Fraud and Abuse; (5) Health Centers; (6) Health Workforce and the National Health Service Corps; (7) Community-Based Prevention and Wellness; (8) Maternal and Child Health; (9) Long-Term Care; (10) Comparative Effectiveness Research; (11) Biomedical Research; and (12) ACA Implementation: Administrative Expenses.

Each table row gives information on a specific ACA provision, organized across four columns. The first column shows the ACA section or subsection number. The second column indicates whether the provision is *freestanding* (i.e., new statutory authority that is not amending an existing statute) or *amendatory* (i.e., amends an existing statute, typically the Social Security Act). Amendatory provisions either add a new program to the statute or modify an existing one. The third column gives a brief description of the program or activity, including details of the appropriation or fund transfer. The entry also includes the name of the administering agency within HHS and, if applicable, the Catalog of Federal Domestic Assistance (CFDA) number for the grant program.[6] The fourth column shows the amount of obligations to date, based on information in the HHS Tracking Accountability in Government Grants System (TAGGS), unless specified otherwise. The TAGGS database is a central repository for grants awarded by all the HHS operating divisions (agencies) and several offices within the Office of the Secretary. It is updated daily with new data provided by these entities.[7]

Appropriations Vary by Duration and Amount

In many instances the ACA provided *annual appropriations* of specified amounts for one or more fiscal years. These funds must be obligated during the fiscal year in which the funds become available for obligation. A few provisions are *multiple-year appropriations*, in which the amount appropriated is available for obligation for a period of time in excess of one fiscal year (e.g., for the period FY2011 through FY2014). Often the provision includes additional language stating that the funds are to remain available "until expended" or "without fiscal year limitation."

Most ACA appropriations and fund transfers are for a limited time period. Some programs received a single annual appropriation, often with the stipulation that the funds remain available

---

[5] CRS Report R41390, *Discretionary Spending Under the Affordable Care Act (ACA)*, coordinated by C. Stephen Redhead.

[6] CFDA is a government-wide compendium of federal grant and other assistance programs. Each program is assigned a unique five-digit number, XX.XXX, where the first two digits represent the funding agency and the second three digits represent the program. Programs funded by the Department of Health and Human Services begin with the number 93. For more information, see https://www.cfda.gov.

[7] To access and search the TAGGS database, go to http://www.taggs hhs.gov/.

until expended. Others were provided funding through FY2014 or FY2015, or in some cases through FY2019. The ACA included four provisions (i.e., Sections 3021(a), 3403, 10323(b), and 4002) that continue to provide annual or multiple-year appropriations beyond FY2019 in perpetuity.

The ACA also included three *indefinite* appropriations that provide an unspecified amount of funding as indicated by the phrase "such sums as may be necessary," or SSAN. One such provision (i.e., Section 1311) appropriated SSAN and authorized the HHS Secretary to determine the specific amount necessary for the grant program.[8]

Table 2 provides additional details on each of the appropriations (and fund transfers) summarized in **Table 1**. It shows the amount available for obligation in each fiscal year (or multi-year period) over the 10-year period FY2010 through FY2019. Note that the provisions are organized and grouped under the same headings used in **Table 1**. The final column in **Table 2** ("Total") shows for each provision the total amount of appropriations or fund transfers. Note that in several cases the total amount has yet to be determined (see table entries for Sections 1311, 3403, 6301(d) & (e), 9023(e), and 10323(a)). For three of the provisions that continue to provide funding beyond FY2019, the amount in the total column represents the cumulative amount appropriated through FY2019 (see table entries for Sections 3021(a), 4002, and 10323(b)). Unless otherwise stated, references to the Secretary in both tables refer to the HHS Secretary. A list of the federal laws and agencies referred to in this report by their acronym is provided in **Appendix A**.

Numerous Programs Have Received ACA Funding

As summarized in the tables, the ACA funded a broad range of new and existing programs. The law appropriated significant amounts to support the following short-term health care programs for targeted groups prior to the health insurance exchanges becoming operational in 2014: (1) $5 billion for the Pre-Existing Condition Insurance Plan (PCIP), a temporary insurance program to provide health insurance coverage for uninsured individuals with a pre-existing condition; (2) $5 billion for a temporary reinsurance program to reimburse employers for a portion of the costs of providing health benefits to early retirees aged 55-64; and (3) $6 billion for the Consumer Operated and Oriented Plan (CO-OP) program, to support temporary health insurance cooperatives. The ACA appropriated $2.4 billion for maternal and child health programs and provided an unspecified amount of funding for state grants to plan and establish health insurance exchanges.[9]

The law established the Center for Medicare and Medicaid Innovation (CMMI) within the Centers for Medicare and Medicaid Services (CMS) and appropriated $10 billion for the FY2011-FY2019 period—and $10 billion for each subsequent 10-year period—for CMMI to test and implement innovative payment and service delivery models. It also established and funded an Independent Payment Advisory Board (IPAB) to make recommendations to Congress for achieving specific Medicare spending reductions if costs exceed a target growth rate. IPAB's

---

[8] The two other indefinite appropriations (i.e., Sections 5508(c), and 9023(e)) provide SSAN to carry out a program, but in each case there is an upper limit on the amount that may be appropriated. Note that a fourth provision (i.e., Section 10323(a)) requires the HHS Secretary to transfer SSAN from the Medicare trust funds to carry out a pilot program.

[9] For a state-by-state breakdown of ACA exchange planning and establishment grants, see CRS Report R43066, *Federal Funding for Health Insurance Exchanges*, by Annie L. Mach and C. Stephen Redhead.

recommendations are to take effect unless Congress overrides them, in which case Congress would be responsible for achieving the same level of savings.

The ACA created four special funds and appropriated substantial amounts to each one:

- The **Community Health Center Fund (CHCF)**, to which the ACA appropriated a total of $11 billion in annual appropriations over the five-year period FY2011-FY2015), is helping support the federal health centers program and the National Health Service Corps (NHSC). [Note: A separate ACA appropriation provided $1.5 billion for health center construction and renovation.] While CHCF funding may have been intended to supplement annual discretionary appropriations for the health centers program and the NHSC, the funds have partially supplanted (i.e., replaced) discretionary health center funding and have become the sole source of funding for the NHSC program, which received no discretionary funds in FY2012, FY2013, or FY2014.[10]

- The **Prevention and Public Health Fund (PPHF)**, for which the ACA provided a permanent annual appropriation, is intended to support prevention, wellness, and other public health-related programs and activities authorized under the Public Health Service Act (PHSA).[11] PPHF funds have been used to support several new discretionary grant programs authorized by the ACA. The funds are also supplementing, and in some cases supplanting, annual discretionary appropriations for a number of established programs, including ones that were reauthorized by the ACA. In FY2013, almost half of the PPHF funds were used to help pay for CMS's administrative costs associated with exchange operations.[12]

- The **Patient-Centered Outcomes Research Trust Fund (PCORTF)** is supporting comparative effectiveness research with a mix of annual appropriations—some of which are offset by revenues from a fee imposed on private health plans—and transfers from the Medicare Part A and Part B trust funds through FY2019.

- The **Health Insurance Reform Implementation Fund (HIRIF)**, to which the ACA appropriated $1 billion, is helping cover the administrative costs of implementing the law.

Overall, the law included more than $100 billion in direct appropriations over the 10-year period FY2010-FY2019, including $40 billion to provide CHIP funding for FY2014 and FY2015.

Congress Has Extended and Rescinded Some ACA Funding

As already noted, most of the ACA funding is for a limited period of time. Three laws enacted since 2012 have extended funding for some programs whose ACA funding was (or is) about to

---

[10] For more information, see CRS Report R42433, *Federal Health Centers*, by Elayne J. Heisler; and CRS Report R41390, *Discretionary Spending Under the Affordable Care Act (ACA)*, coordinated by C. Stephen Redhead.

[11] Section 3205 of the Middle Class Tax Relief and Job Creation Act of 2012 (P.L. 112-96, 126 Stat. 156) reduced the ACA's annual appropriations to the PPHF over the period FY2013-FY2021 by a total of $6.25 billion. See **Table 1**.

[12] For more information, see CRS Report R41390, *Discretionary Spending Under the Affordable Care Act (ACA)*, coordinated by C. Stephen Redhead.

lapse. Those laws are the American Taxpayer Relief Act of 2012 (ATRA),[13] the Pathway for SGR Reform Act of 2013 (PSGRRA),[14] and the Protecting Access to Medicare Act of 2014 (PAMA).[15]

Lawmakers opposed to specific ACA provisions have also succeeded in getting some ACA funding rescinded. ATRA, the Middle Class Tax Relief and Job Creation Act of 2012, and enacted appropriations acts for each of the past four fiscal years (i.e., FY2011, FY2012, FY2013, and FY2014) have all included ACA funding rescissions.[16]

All the ACA funding extensions and rescissions are summarized in the tables.

Impact of Sequestration on ACA Mandatory Spending

Federal outlays on insurance expansion coverage under the ACA, which constitute most of the mandatory spending under the ACA, are almost entirely exempt from the annual sequestration triggered by the Budget Control Act of 2011 (BCA).[17] However, the mandatory appropriations in the ACA are, in general, fully sequestrable at the percentage rate applicable to nonexempt nondefense mandatory spending. For more background on the BCA's annual spending reductions, see **Appendix B**.

The **FY2013** sequestration order reduced spending on nonexempt nondefense mandatory programs by 5.1%. [Note: This percentage reflects adjustments made by ATRA, which reduced the overall dollar amount that needed to be cut from FY2013 defense and nondefense spending.] The **FY2014** sequestration order reduced spending on nonexempt nondefense mandatory programs by 7.2%. Finally, the **FY2015** sequestration order, issued on March 10, 2014, will reduce spending on nonexempt nondefense mandatory programs by 7.3%.

For technical reasons, OMB concluded that cuts in CHCF funding for community health centers and migrant health centers are capped at 2%.

Importantly, only new budget authority for nondefense programs is sequestrable in any given fiscal year. That includes advance appropriations that first become available for obligation in that year. Unobligated balances carried over from previous fiscal years are exempt from sequestration.[18]

---

[13] P.L. 112-240, 126 Stat. 2313.

[14] P.L. 113-67, Division B, 127 Stat. 1195.

[15] P.L. 113-93, 128 Stat. 1040.

[16] For more information on all the legislative actions taken to amend the ACA since its enactment, including actions taken through the annual appropriations process, see CRS Report R43289, *Legislative Actions to Repeal, Defund, or Delay the Affordable Care Act*, by C. Stephen Redhead and Janet Kinzer.

[17] P.L. 112-25, 125 Stat. 240.

[18] The exemption for nondefense unobligated balances is provided in BBEDCA Section 255(e). It reads as follows: "Unobligated balances of budget authority carried over from prior fiscal years, except balances in the defense category, shall be exempt from reduction under any order issued under this part." 2 U.S.C. § 905(e).

The exemption for unobligated balances carried over from prior fiscal years applies to a number of ACA appropriations. As already mentioned, the appropriations provision often specifies that the funds are to remain available "until expended" or "without fiscal year limitation." One example is the PCIP program to provide temporary health insurance coverage for eligible individuals who have been uninsured for six months and have a pre-existing condition. The ACA appropriated $5 billion in FY2010, to remain available without fiscal year limitation, to pay claims against the PCIP that are in excess of the premiums collected from enrollees. Unobligated PCIP funds carried over to FY2013 or FY2014 were exempt from sequestration. Another example is CMMI, which received a $10 billion multiple-year appropriation in FY2011 to remain available for obligation through FY2019.

Table 1. Mandatory Appropriations and Medicare Trust Fund Transfers in the Affordable Care Act

ACA Section	Statutory Authority	Summary of Provision	Obligations as of July 22, 2014, Based on TAGGS Unless Specified Otherwise
Private Health Insurance			
1002	New PHSA Sec. 2793	**Consumer Assistance Program (CAP).** Appropriated $30 million, to remain available without fiscal year limitation, for CAP grants to states to enable them (or the exchanges operating in such states) to establish, expand, or provide support for offices of health insurance consumer assistance, and health insurance ombudsman programs. [CMS/CCIIO; CFDA 93.519]	$40 million Total includes original funding plus awards made using additional funds. See http://www.cms.gov/CCIIO/Programs-and-Initiatives/Consumer-Support-and-Information/Consumer-Assistance-Program-Grants.html.
1003	New PHSA Sec. 2794	**Review of health insurance premium rates.** Appropriated $250 million for grants to states over the five-year period FY2010-FY2014 to support programs that review annual increases in health insurance premiums. No state may receive less than $1 million or more than $5 million in a grant year. Unobligated funds the end of FY2014 are to remain available for grants to states for planning and implementing ACA's individual and group market reforms. [CMS/CCIIO; CFDA 93.511]	$215 million To date, three rounds of rate review grants have been awarded. See http://www.cms.gov/CCIIO/Programs-and-Initiatives/Health-Insurance-Market-Reforms/Review-of-Insurance-Rates.html.
1101	New freestanding authority	**Pre-Existing Condition Insurance Plan (PCIP).** Required the Secretary to establish a temporary program—PCIP—to provide health insurance coverage for eligible individuals who have been uninsured for six months and have a pre-existing condition. Appropriated $5 billion, to remain available without fiscal year limitation, to pay claims against (and administrative costs of) the PCIP program that are in excess of premiums collected from enrollees. Note: Until June 2013, 27 states administered their own PCIP programs; the remaining 23 states and DC elected to have their PCIP program federally administered. Seventeen state-run PCIP programs then transferred administration to the federal program. [CMS/CCIIO; CFDA 93.529]	According to the most recent quarterly update, net PCIP outlays through September 2013 totaled $3.956 billion. More than 134,000 individuals have received coverage under PCIP. Originally scheduled to end on January 1, 2014, the program was extended through March 31, 2014. However, the federally-run PCIP and the state-based PCIPs stopped accepting new enrollees on February 16, 2013, and March 2, 2013, respectively, because of the limited amount of funding. See http://www.cms.gov/CCIIO/Programs-and-Initiatives/Insurance-Programs/Pre-Existing-Condition-Insurance-Plan.html; and https://www.pcip.gov.
1102	New freestanding authority	**Early Retiree Reinsurance Program (ERRP).** Required the Secretary to establish a temporary ERRP to provide reimbursement to participating employer-based plans for a portion of the cost of providing health benefits to early retirees age 55-64 and their families. Appropriated $5 billion, to remain available without fiscal year limitation, to carry out the ERRP. [CMS/CCIIO]	According to the most recent program update, ERRP outlays through February 2012 totaled $4.725 billion. ERRP has provided payments to more than 2,800 employers and other sponsors of retiree plans. The program ended on January 1, 2014; however, HHS stopped accepting new ERRP applications on May 5, 2011, because of limited funding. See http://www.cms.gov/CCIIO/Programs-and-Initiatives/Insurance-Programs/Early-Retiree-Reinsurance-Program.html; and http://www.errp.gov.

ACA Section	Statutory Authority	Summary of Provision	Obligations as of July 22, 2014, Based on TAGGS Unless Specified Otherwise
1311	New freestanding authority	**Health insurance exchange grants.** Appropriated to the Secretary an amount necessary to award exchange planning and establishment grants to states. Instructs the Secretary each fiscal year to determine the total amount to be made available. No grants may be awarded after January 1, 2015, by which time exchanges must be self-sustaining. [CMS/CCIIO; CFDA 93.525]	$4.755 billion For more information on federal funding for health insurance exchanges, see CRS Report R43066, *Federal Funding for Health Insurance Exchanges.*
1322	New freestanding authority	**Consumer Operated and Oriented Plan (CO-OP).** Required the Secretary to establish the CO-OP program to provide low-interest loans until July 1, 2013, for the creation of nonprofit member-run health insurance issuers that offer qualified health plans in the individual and small group markets. Appropriated $6 billion to carry out the CO-OP program. Note: The FY2011 and FY2012 Labor-HHS-Education appropriations acts (P.L. 112-10 and P.L. 112-74, respectively) together rescinded a total of $2.6 billion of the original appropriation. The American Taxpayer Relief Act of 2012 (ATRA; P.L. 112-240) rescinded 90% of the program's unobligated balance as of January 2, 2013, and transferred the remaining unobligated funds to a new CO-OP contingency fund to provide assistance and oversight to CO-OP loan recipients, ending CMS's authority to make new loans. Overall, Congress rescinded a total of $4.879 billion, leaving $1.121 billion of the original $6 billion CO-OP program appropriation. [CMS/CCIIO]	According to a December 13, 2013, fact sheet, the CO-OP program has awarded a total of $2.103 billion in loans to 23 nonprofits that plan to offer coverage in a total of 26 states. See http://www.cms.gov/CCIIO/Programs-and-Initiatives/Insurance-Programs/Consumer-Operated-and-Oriented-Plan-Program.html.
1323	New freestanding authority	**Funding for territories.** Appropriated $1 billion, available for the period FY2014-FY2019, for U.S. territories that elect to establish a health insurance exchange. Funds must be used to provide premium and cost-sharing assistance to territory residents who obtain health insurance coverage through the exchange.	No public information located on funding obligations.
Medicaid and State Children's Health Insurance Program (CHIP)			
2701	New SSA Sec. 1139B	**Medicaid adult health quality measures.** Required the Secretary to develop and, not later than January 1, 2012, publish an initial core set of quality measures for Medicaid-eligible adults. Appropriated $60 million for each of FY2010-FY2014, to remain available until expended. Total amount = $300 million. Note: The Protecting Access to Medicare Act of 2014 (PAMA; P.L. 113-93) requires $15 million of these funds to be used for the development of quality measures for children enrolled in Medicaid and CHIP, pursuant to SSA Sec. 1139A. [CMS; CFDA 93.609]	$49 million See http://www.medicaid.gov/Medicaid-CHIP-Program-Information/By-Topics/Quality-of-Care/Adult-Health-Care-Quality-Measures.html.
2707	New freestanding authority	**Medicaid emergency psychiatric demonstration program.** Appropriated $75 million for FY2011, to remain available for obligation through December 2015, for a three-year demonstration in which eligible states are required to reimburse certain institutions for mental disease (IMDs) for services provided to Medicaid beneficiaries aged 21 through 64 who are in need of medical assistance to stabilize an emergency psychiatric condition. [CMS/CMI; CFDA 93.537]	Eleven states plus DC are participating in the demonstration, which began in July 2012. No public information located on funding obligations. See http://innovation.cms.gov/initiatives/Medicaid-Emergency-Psychiatric-Demo/.

ACA Section	Statutory Authority	Summary of Provision	Obligations as of July 22, 2014, Based on TAGGS Unless Specified Otherwise
2801	Amends SSA Sec. 1900	**Medicaid and CHIP Payment and Access Commission (MACPAC).** Clarified and expanded MACPAC's duties; for example, to include a review and assessment of payment policies under Medicaid and CHIP and how factors affecting expenditures and payment methodologies enable beneficiaries to obtain services, affect provider supply, and affect providers that serve a disproportionate share of low-income and other vulnerable populations. Appropriated $9 million and transferred from CHIP funding an additional $2 million for FY2010. Total amount = $11 million, to remain available until expended.	ACA funding was obligated in FY2011 and FY2012. See http://www.macpac.gov/.
4108	New freestanding authority	**Medicaid Incentives for the Prevention of Chronic Diseases (MIPCD).** Required the Secretary to award five-year grants to states, subject to annual renewal of funding, to provide incentives for Medicaid beneficiaries to participate in evidence-based healthy lifestyle programs to prevent or help manage chronic disease. Appropriated $100 million for the five-year period beginning January 1, 2011, to remain available until expended. [CMS/CMI; CFDA 93.536]	$51 million MIPCD grants have been awarded to 10 states. See http://www.innovations.cms.gov/initiatives/MIPCD/index.html.
4306	Amends SSA Sec. 1139A(e)	**CHIP childhood obesity demonstration program.** Appropriated $25 million for the period FY2010 through FY2014 for a program authorized by the Children's Health Insurance Program Reauthorization Act of 2009 (CHIPRA; P.L. 111-3), which requires the Secretary to conduct a demonstration project to develop a model for reducing childhood obesity. [CDC; CFDA 93.535]	$24 million Funding has been awarded to three research facilities to identify effective childhood obesity prevention strategies, and to a fourth facility to evaluate the strategies and share successes. See http://www.cdc.gov/obesity/childhood/researchproject.html.
10203(d)	Amends SSA Secs. 2104 & 2113	**CHIP annual appropriations, and outreach and enrollment grants.** Appropriated funding for the CHIP program for FY2014 ($19.147 billion) and FY2015 ($21.061 billion); the program previously had been funded through FY2013. Also, extended the time period for the Connecting Kids to Coverage Outreach and Enrollment grants through FY2015 and increased the existing appropriation for such grants from $100 million to $140 million. [CMS; CFDA 93.767]	Since 2009, CMS has awarded three cycles of outreach and enrollment grants totaling $122 million to states, local governments, community organizations, and tribal organizations. See http://www.insurekidsnow.gov/professionals/outreach/grantees/index.html.

ACA Section	Statutory Authority	Summary of Provision	Obligations as of July 22, 2014, Based on TAGGS Unless Specified Otherwise
Medicare			
3014	Amends SSA Sec. 1890(b). New SSA Sec. 1890A	**Medicare quality and efficiency measures.** Expanded the duties of the consensus-based entity under contract with CMS pursuant to SSA Sec. 1890 (currently the National Quality Forum). Required the entity to convene multi-stakeholder groups to provide input on the national priorities for health care quality improvement (developed under the ACA). In addition, the multi-stakeholder groups are required to provide input on the selection of quality measures for use in various specified Medicare payment systems for hospitals and other providers, as well as in other health care programs, and for use in reporting performance information to the public. Established a multi-step pre-rulemaking process and timeline for the adoption, dissemination, and review of measures by the Secretary. Required the Secretary to transfer from the Medicare Part A and Part B trust funds $20 million for each of FY2010 through FY2014, to remain available until expended.[a] Total amount = $100 million. [CMS]	No public information located on funding obligations.
3021(a)	New SSA Sec. 1115A	**Center for Medicare and Medicaid Innovation (CMMI).** Required the Secretary, no later than January 1, 2011, to establish the CMMI within CMS. The purpose of CMMI is to test and evaluate innovative payment and service delivery models to reduce program expenditures under Medicare, Medicaid, and CHIP while preserving or enhancing the quality of care furnished under these programs. In selecting the models, the Secretary is also required to give preference to those that improve the coordination, quality, and efficiency of health care services. Appropriated (1) $5 million for FY2010 for the selection, testing, and evaluation of new payment and service delivery models; and (2) $10 billion for the period FY2011 through FY2019, plus $10 billion for each subsequent 10-year period, to continue such activities and for the expansion and nationwide implementation of successful models. Amounts are to remain available until expended.[b] [CMS]	According to CMS's budget documents (FY2013-FY2015), CMMI's obligations are as follows: FY2011 (actual) = $95 million; FY2012 (actual) = $781 million; FY2013 (actual) = $953 million; FY2014 (current law) = $1.637 billion; FY2015 (estimate) = $1.522 billion. For information on CMI's programs, which include several of the initiatives summarized in this table, see http://www.innovations.cms.gov/.
3024	New SSA Sec. 1866E	**Medicare independence at home demonstration program.** Required the Secretary to conduct a three-year Medicare demonstration program, beginning no later than January 1, 2012, to test a payment incentive and service delivery model that uses physician- and nurse practitioner-directed primary care teams to provide home-based services to chronically ill patients. The Secretary must submit a plan, no later than January 1, 2016, for expanding the program if it is determined that such expansion would improve the quality of care and reduce spending. Required the Secretary to transfer from the Medicare Part A and Part B trust funds $5 million for each of FY2010 through FY2015 for administering and carrying out the demonstration, to remain available until expended.[a] Total amount = $30 million. [CMS]	Fourteen independent practices and three consortia are participating in the independence at home demonstration, administered by CMMI. No public information located on funding obligations. See http://innovation.cms.gov/initiatives/Independence-at-Home/index.html.

ACA Section	Statutory Authority	Summary of Provision	Obligations as of July 22, 2014, Based on TAGGS Unless Specified Otherwise
3026	New freestanding authority	**Community-based Care Transitions Program (CCTP).** Required the Secretary to establish a five-year program, beginning January 1, 2011, to provide funding to eligible hospitals and community-based organizations to test models for improving care transitions from the hospital to other settings for high-risk Medicare beneficiaries. Required the Secretary to transfer from the Medicare Part A and Part B trust funds $500 million for the period FY2011 through FY2015, to remain available until expended.[a] Note: The FY2013 Labor-HHS-Education appropriations act (P.L. 113-6) rescinded $200 million of CCTP's transfer. [CMS]	There are currently 102 organizations participating in the CCTP, which is administered by CMMI as part of the Partnership for Patients initiative. No public information located on funding obligations. See http://www.innovations.cms.gov/initiatives/CCTP/.
3027(b)	Amends DRA Sec. 5007	**Medicare hospital gainsharing demonstration program.** CMS is supporting two projects that allow hospitals to provide gainsharing payments to physicians that represent a share of the savings incurred as a result of collaborative efforts to improve overall quality and efficiency. The ACA appropriated $1.6 million for FY2010, to remain available through FY2014 or until expended, for carrying out the demonstration. [CMS]	There are two hospitals participating in the gainsharing demonstration, which is administered by CMMI. No public information located on funding obligations. See http://innovation.cms.gov/initiatives/Medicare-Hospital-Gainsharing/.
3113	New freestanding authority	**Diagnostic laboratory test demonstration program.** Required the Secretary to conduct a two-year demonstration program beginning July 1, 2011, with a subsequent report to Congress, to test the impact of direct payments for certain complex laboratory tests on Medicare costs and quality of care. Payments are to be made from the Part B trust fund and may not exceed $100 million. Transferred $5 million from the Medicare Part B trust fund, to remain available until expended, for carrying out the demonstration program and preparing the subsequent report. [CMS]	Payments under the demonstration began in January 2012. See http://www.cms.gov/Medicare/Demonstration-Projects/DemoProjectsEvalRpts/Downloads/TCCDLT_FactSheet.pdf.
3306	Amends MIPPA Sec. 119	**Outreach and assistance for Medicare low-income programs.** Transferred a total of $45 million from the Medicare Part A and Part B trust funds for the period FY2010 through FY2012 to extend funding for the following beneficiary outreach and education activities for Medicare low-income programs that were funded by the Medicare Improvements for Patients and Providers Act of 2008 (MIPPA; P.L. 110-275): (1) State Health Insurance Counseling and Assistance Programs (SHIPs), $15 million; (2) Area Agencies on Aging (AAAs), $15 million; (3) Aging and Disability Resource Centers (ADRCs), $10 million; and (4) the National Center for Benefits Outreach and Enrollment (NCBOE), $5 million. Note: ATRA (P.L. 112-240) transferred $25 million for FY2013 for these programs: (1) SHIPs, $7.5 million; (2) AAAs, $7.5 million; (3) ADRCs, $5 million; and (4) NCBOE, $5 million. The Pathway for SGR Reform Act of 2013 (PSGRRA; P.L. 113-67, Division B) transferred $12.5 million to provide prorated funding for the first half of FY2014. PAMA (P.L. 113-93) amended PSGRRA by transferring $25 million for FY2014 (same as FY2013) and by transferring $12.5 million for the first half of FY2015. Funds are to remain available until expended.[c] [ACL, CMS; CFDA 93.071]	$41 million (FY2009-FY2014)

ACA Section	Statutory Authority	Summary of Provision	Obligations as of July 22, 2014, Based on TAGGS Unless Specified Otherwise
3403	New SSA Sec. 1899A	**Independent Payment Advisory Board (IPAB).** Established an independent, 15-member advisory board tasked with presenting Congress with comprehensive proposals to reduce excess cost growth and improve quality of care for Medicare beneficiaries. Appropriated $15 million for FY2012 to support the board's activities. For each subsequent fiscal year, appropriates the amount from the previous fiscal year adjusted for inflation. Sixty percent of the appropriation is to be derived by transfer from the Medicare Part A trust fund, and 40% is to be derived by transfer from the Medicare Part B trust fund. Note: The Labor-HHS-Education appropriations acts for FY2012, FY2013 and FY2014 (P.L. 112-74, P.L. 113-6, and P.L. 113-76, respectively) each rescinded $10 million of IPAB's appropriation for that fiscal year.	The President has not appointed, nor has the Senate approved, any IPAB members.
4202(b)	New freestanding authority	**Medicare prevention and wellness evaluation.** Transferred $50 million from the Medicare Part A and Part B trust funds, to remain available until expended, to fund an evaluation of community-based prevention and wellness programs and, based on the findings, develop a plan to promote healthy lifestyles and chronic disease self-management among Medicare beneficiaries.[a] [CMS]	No public information located on funding obligations.
4204(e)	New freestanding authority	**Medicare vaccine coverage.** Appropriated $1 million for FY2010 for a GAO report on the impact of Medicare Part D vaccine coverage on access to those vaccines among beneficiaries.	Report released in December 2011 (GAO-12-61).
10323(a)	New SSA Sec. 1881A	**Environmental health hazards.** Extended Medicare eligibility to individuals with specified health conditions linked to environmental exposures, who have resided for specified times in an area subject to a Superfund public health emergency declaration. Required the Secretary to establish a pilot program, with appropriate reimbursement methodologies, to provide comprehensive, coordinated, and cost-effective care to such individuals. Transferred such sums as may be necessary from the Medicare Part A and Part B trust funds to carry out the pilot program.[a] [CMS]	No public information located on funding obligations.
10323(b)	New SSA Sec. 2009	**Environmental health hazards.** Appropriated $23 million for the period FY2010 through FY2014, and $20 million for each five-year period thereafter, for grants to state and local government agencies, health care facilities, and other entities to (1) provide screening for specified lung diseases and other environmental health conditions to individuals who have resided for specified times in an area subject to a Superfund public health emergency declaration; and (2) disseminate public information about the availability of screening, the detection and treatment of environmental health conditions, and the availability of Medicare benefits to certain individuals diagnosed with such conditions, pursuant to new SSA Sec. 1881A (as added by ACA Sec. 10323(a)). [CMS; CFDA 93.534]	$10 million Funding provided for an asbestos health screening program in Libby, Montana.

ACA Section	Statutory Authority	Summary of Provision	Obligations as of July 22, 2014, Based on TAGGS Unless Specified Otherwise
Fraud and Abuse			
6402(i) & HCERA Sec. 1303(a)	Amends SSA Sec. 1817(k)	**Health Care Fraud and Abuse Control (HCFAC) Account.** Applied a permanent inflation adjustment to the annual appropriation (provided under SSA Sec. 1817(k)) for the HCFAC account. Appropriated from the Medicare Part A trust fund the following supplemental amounts for the HCFAC account: $10 million for each of FY2011 through FY2020; plus an additional $95 million for FY2011, $55 million for FY2012, $30 million for each of FY2013 and FY2014, and $20 million for each of FY2015 and FY2016. Total amount = $350 million. Funds are to remain available until expended. [CMS]	No public information located on ACA funding obligations.
Health Centers			
4101(a)	New freestanding authority	**School-based health centers (SBHCs).** Appropriated $50 million for each of FY2010 through FY2013, to remain available until expended, for a grant program to fund the construction and renovation of school-based health centers. Total amount = $200 million. [HRSA; CFDA 93.501]	$140 million See http://bphc.hrsa.gov/about/schoolbased/index.html.
10503(b)(1)	New freestanding authority	**Community-based health centers.** Transferred from the CHCF the following amounts for health center operations, to remain available until expended: FY2011 = $1 billion; FY2012 = $1.2 billion; FY2013 = $1.5 billion; FY2014 = $2.2 billion; and FY2015 = $3.6 billion. Total amount = $9.5 billion. [HRSA; CFDA 93.527]	According to the Budget Appendices for FY2013-FY2015, the obligations of ACA funds for health centers are as follows: FY2011 (actual) = $998 million; FY2012 (actual) = $1.171 billion; FY2013 (actual) = $1.491 billion; FY2014 (actual) = $2.145 billion; FY2015 (estimate) = $3.600 billion. See http://bphc.hrsa.gov/about/healthcenterfactsheet.pdf.
10503(c)	New freestanding authority	**Health center construction and renovation.** Appropriated $1.5 billion, to be available for the period FY2011 through FY2015, and to remain available until expended, for health center construction and renovation. [HRSA; CFDA 93.526]	$1.486 billion
Health Workforce and the National Health Service Corps			
10503(b)(2)	New freestanding authority	**National Health Service Corps (NHSC).** Transfers from the CHCF the following amounts for NHSC operations, scholarships, and loan repayments, to remain available until expended: FY2011 = $290 million; FY2012 = $295 million; FY2013 = $300 million; FY2014 = $305 million; and FY2015 = $310 million. Total amount = $1.5 billion. [HRSA; CFDA 93.547]	According to the Budget Appendices for FY2013-FY2015, the obligations of ACA funds for the NHSC are as follows: FY2011 (actual) = $289 million; FY2012 (actual) = $297 million; FY2013 (actual) = $286 million; FY2014 (estimate) = $283 million; FY2015 (estimate) = $310 million.

ACA Section	Statutory Authority	Summary of Provision	Obligations as of July 22, 2014, Based on TAGGS Unless Specified Otherwise
5507(a)	New SSA Sec. 2008	**Health workforce demonstration programs.** Required the Secretary to establish two demonstration projects. The first is to award health profession opportunity grants to states, Indian tribes, institutions of higher education, and local workforce investment boards to help low-income individuals obtain education and training in health care jobs that pay well and are in high demand. Funds may be used to provide financial aid and other supportive services. The second project is to provide states with grants to develop core training competencies and certification programs for personal and home care aides. Appropriated $85 million for each of FY2010 through FY2014, of which $5 million in each of FY2010 through FY2012 is to be used for the second project. Total amount = $425 million. Note: PAMA (P.L. 113-93) provided an additional year of funding (i.e., $85 million for FY2015). [ACF, HRSA; CFDA 93.093, 93.512]	$264 million: Health Profession Opportunity Grant (HPOG) $13 million: Personal and Home Care Aide State Training (PHCAST) program See http://www.acf.hhs.gov/programs/ofa/programs/hpog; and http://bhpr.hrsa.gov/nursing/grants/phcast.html.
5507(b)	Amends SSA Sec. 501(c)	**Family-to-family health information centers.** Renewed funding for the family-to-family information centers, which assist families of children with disabilities or special health care needs and the professionals who serve them, by appropriating $5 million for each of FY2010 through FY2012, to remain available until expended. Total amount = $15 million. Note: ATRA (P.L. 112-240) appropriated $5 million for FY2013; PSGRRA (P.L. 113-67, Division B) appropriated $2.5 million for the first half of FY2014; and PAMA (P.L. 113-93) appropriated $2.5 million for the second half of FY2014 and $2.5 million for the first half of FY2015. [HRSA; CFDA 93.504]	$11 million (FY2012-FY2014) See http://mchb.hrsa.gov/programs/familytofamily/index.html.
5508(c)	New PHSA Sec. 340H	**Teaching health centers.** Appropriated such sums as may be necessary, not to exceed $230 million, for the period FY2011 through FY2015 to make payments for direct and indirect graduate medical education (GME) costs to qualified teaching health centers (THCs). [HRSA; CFDA 93.530]	$99 million See http://bhpr.hrsa.gov/grants/teachinghealthcenters/.
5509	New freestanding authority	**Medicare graduate nurse education demonstration program.** Appropriated $50 million for each of FY2012 through FY2015, to remain available until expended, for a Medicare demonstration program under which up to five eligible hospitals will receive reimbursement for providing advanced practice nurses with clinical training in primary care, preventive care, transitional care, and chronic care management. Total amount = $200 million. [CMS/CMI]	CMMI, which is administering this program, selected five participating hospitals and has begun making reimbursement payments. See http://innovations.cms.gov/initiatives/GNE/index.html.
10502	New freestanding authority	**Health care facility construction.** Appropriated $100 million for FY2010, to remain available for obligation until Sept. 30, 2011, for debt service on, or construction or renovation of, a hospital affiliated with a state's sole public medical and dental school. [HRSA; CFDA 93.502]	$100 million Funding awarded to Ohio State University.

ACA Section	Statutory Authority	Summary of Provision	Obligations as of July 22, 2014, Based on TAGGS Unless Specified Otherwise
Community-Based Prevention and Wellness			
4002	New freestanding authority	**Prevention and Public Health Fund (PPHF).** Established a PPHF and originally provided a permanent annual appropriation to the fund, as follows: FY2010 = $500 million; FY2011 = $750 million; FY2012 = $1 billion; FY2013 = $1.25 billion; FY2014 = $1.5 billion; FY2015 and each year thereafter = $2 billion. Required the Secretary to transfer amounts from the fund to HHS accounts to increase funding, over the FY2008 level, for PHSA-authorized prevention, wellness, and public health activities, including prevention research and health screenings. Provided House and Senate appropriators with the authority to transfer monies from the PPHF to eligible activities. Note: The Middle Class Tax Relief and Job Creation Act of 2012 (P.L. 112-96) reduced the annual appropriations to the PPHF over the period FY2013-FY2021 as follows: FY2013 through FY2017 = $1 billion; FY2018 and FY2019 = $1.25 billion; FY2020 and FY2021 = $1.5 billion; FY2022 and each year thereafter = $2 billion. [OS, CDC, HRSA, SAMHSA, ACL; CFDA 93.507, 93.521, 93.522, 93.523, 93.524, 93.531, 93.533, 93.538, 93.539, 93.540, 93.542.]	PPHF funds are annual appropriations that must be obligated during the fiscal year in which they are made available. For an analysis and complete list of all PPHF awards for FY2010 and FY2011, see the GAO report, *Prevention and Public Health Fund: Activities Funded in Fiscal Years 2010 and 2011* (GAO-12-788), at http://www.gao.gov/assets/650/648310.pdf. For a summary of the allocation of PPHF funds for FY2012, FY2013 and FY2014, by agency and program, see http://www.hhs.gov/open/recordsandreports/prevention/index.html. The listed CFDA programs do not capture all the uses of PPHF funding. PPHF funds have also been integrated into existing programs that do not mention PPHF.
Maternal and Child Health			
2951	New SSA Sec. 511	**Maternal, infant, and early childhood home visiting program.** Appropriated the following amounts for grants to states, U.S. territories, and Indian tribes to develop and implement early childhood home visiting programs that adhere to evidence-based models of service delivery: FY2010 = $100 million; FY2011 = $250 million, FY2012 = $350 million; FY2013 = $400 million; FY2014 = $400 million. Total amount = $1.5 billion. Programs must establish benchmarks to measure improvements for the participating families in maternal and newborn health; prevention of child abuse or neglect or child injuries; school readiness and achievement; reductions in crime or domestic violence; family economic self-sufficiency; and coordination and referrals for other community resources and supports. Note: PAMA (P.L. 113-93) appropriated $400 million for the first half of FY2015. [HRSA, ACF; CFDA 93.505, 93.508]	$1.071 billion See http://mchb.hrsa.gov/programs/homevisiting/.

ACA Section	Statutory Authority	Summary of Provision	Obligations as of July 22, 2014, Based on TAGGS Unless Specified Otherwise
2953	New SSA Sec. 513	**Personal Responsibility Education Program (PREP).** Established a state formula grant program to support evidence-based PREPs designed to educate adolescents about abstinence, contraception, and adulthood. Also, required the Secretary to award grants to implement innovative youth pregnancy prevention strategies and to target services at high-risk populations. Appropriated $75 million for each of FY2010 through FY2014, of which $10 million each year is to be reserved for the youth pregnancy prevention grants. Total amount = $375 million. Funds are to remain available until expended. Note: PAMA (P.L. 113-93) appropriated $75 million for FY2015. [ACF; CFDA 93.092]	$303 million See http://www.acf.hhs.gov/programs/fysb/programs/ adolescent-pregnancy-prevention/programs/prep-competitive.
2954	Amends SSA Sec. 510	**Abstinence education grants.** Renewed funding for the state formula grant program to support abstinence education programs by appropriating $50 million for each of FY2010 through FY2014. Total amount = $250 million. Funds are awarded to states based on the proportion of low-income children in each state compared to the national total, and may only be used for teaching abstinence. Note: PAMA (P.L. 113-93) appropriated $50 million for FY2015. [ACF, CDC; CFDA 93.235]	$156 million (FY2010-FY2014) See http://www.acf.hhs.gov/programs/fysb/resource/aegp-fact-sheet.
10211-10214	New freestanding authority	**Pregnancy assistance grants.** Appropriated $25 million for each of FY2010 through FY2019 (total amount = $250 million) to establish a Pregnancy Assistance Fund for the purpose of awarding grants to states to assist pregnant and parenting teens and women. State grantees have the flexibility to make funds available to institutions of higher education, high schools and community service centers, and to the state attorneys general to improve services for pregnant women who are victims of domestic violence, sexual assault, or stalking. [OS; CFDA 93.500]	$89 million See http://www.hhs.gov/ash/oah/oah-initiatives/paf/home.html.
Long-Term Care			
2403	Amends DRA Sec. 6071(h)	**Medicaid Money Follows the Person (MFP) demonstration program.** Extended funding for the MFP demonstration through FY2016. The program authorizes the Secretary to award competitive grants to states to reduce their reliance on institutional care for people needing long-term care, and expand options for elderly people and individuals with disabilities to receive home and community-based long-term care services. Appropriated $450 million for each of FY2012 through FY2016, to remain available through FY2016. Total amount = $2.25 billion. [CMS; CFDA 93.791]	$1.563 billion (FY2007-FY2014) See http://www.medicaid.gov/Medicaid-CHIP-Program-Information/By-Topics/Long-Term-Services-and-Supports/ Balancing/Money-Follows-the-Person.html.

ACA Section	Statutory Authority	Summary of Provision	Obligations as of July 22, 2014, Based on TAGGS Unless Specified Otherwise
2405	New freestanding authority	**State Aging and Disability Resource Centers (ADRCs).** Appropriated $10 million for each of FY2010 through FY2014 (total amount = $50 million) for ADRCs, authorized under OAA Sec. 202. ADRCs serve as a single, coordinated resource for consumer information on the range of long-term care options in community and institutional settings. Some ADRCs also serve as the entry point to publicly administered long-term care programs (e.g., Medicaid, OAA services, state assistance programs). Over 500 ADRC sites have been established across 50 states, DC, and two territories. See also the entry for ACA Sec. 3306, above. [ACL; CFDA 93.517]	$21 million (FY2010-FY2014; includes ACA mandatory + discretionary funds) See http://www.acl.gov/Programs/CDAP/OIP/ADRC/index.aspx.
6201	New freestanding authority	**Background checks of long-term care providers.** Required the Secretary to establish a nationwide program for background checks on direct patient access employees of long-term care facilities or providers, and to provide federal matching funds to states to conduct these activities. Required the Treasury Secretary to transfer to HHS an amount, not to exceed $160 million, specified by the HHS Secretary as necessary to carry out the program for the period FY2010 through FY2012. Funds are to remain available until expended. [CMS; CFDA 93.506]	$57 million
8002(d)	Amends DRA Sec. 6021(d)	**National Clearinghouse for Long-Term Care Information.** Appropriated $3 million for each of FY2011 through FY2015 for the National Clearinghouse for Long-Term Care Information, and required the Clearinghouse to include information on the Community Living Assistance Services and Supports (CLASS) program, established under ACA Sec. 8002(a). Total amount = $15 million. Note: ATRA (P.L. 112-240) repealed the appropriations for the National Clearinghouse and rescinded all unobligated FY2013 funds (as of January 3, 2013), and repealed the CLASS program. [ACL]	$6 million (FY2011-FY2014) See http://longtermcare.gov/.

Comparative Effectiveness Research

ACA Section	Statutory Authority	Summary of Provision	Obligations as of July 22, 2014, Based on TAGGS Unless Specified Otherwise
6301(d)-(e)	New IRC Secs. 9511, 4375, & 4376. New SSA Sec. 1183	**Patient-Centered Outcomes Research Trust Fund (PCORTF).** Established the PCORTF to fund the new Patient-Centered Outcomes Research Institute (PCORI) and its comparative effectiveness research activities. Appropriated to the PCORTF $10 million for FY2010, $50 million for FY2011, and $150 million for each of FY2012 through FY2019, for a total of $1.26 billion over that 10-year period. For each of FY2013 through FY2019, the PCORTF is to receive additional appropriations equal to the net revenues from a new fee on health insurance policies and self-insured plans,[d] as well as Medicare trust fund transfers.[e] Each fiscal year, 20% of the funds in the PCORTF are to be transferred to the Secretary, to remain available until expended. Of those transferred funds, 80% are to be provided to AHRQ. [OS, AHRQ]	Details of all the PCORI research awards are available at http://www.pcori.org/.

ACA Section	Statutory Authority	Summary of Provision	Obligations as of July 22, 2014, Based on TAGGS Unless Specified Otherwise
Biomedical Research			
9023	New IRC Sec. 48D	**Therapeutic research and development tax credits and grants.** Created a two-year tax credit program, subject to an overall cap of $1 billion, for small companies (250 or fewer employees) that invest in new therapies to prevent, diagnose, and treat cancer and other diseases. Companies could apply for one or more tax credits, each covering up to 50% of the cost of qualifying research investments made in 2009 and 2010. However, the total amount of tax credits any one company receives for the two years could not exceed $5 million. Companies could elect to receive one or more grants in lieu of tax credits, subject to the same restrictions (i.e., grants could cover up to 50% of the cost of qualifying investments made in 2009 and 2010; the total amount of grants any one company receives for the two years could not exceed $5 million). Appropriated such sums as may be necessary to carry out the grant program. [IRS]	According to the IRS: total grant awards = $970 million; total tax credits = $17 million. See http://www.irs.gov/Businesses/Small-Businesses-&-Self-Employed/Qualifying-Therapeutic-Discovery-Project-Credits-and-Grants.
ACA Implementation: Administrative Expenses			
HCERA Sec. 1005	New freestanding authority	**Health Insurance Reform Implementation Fund (HIRIF).** Appropriated $1 billion to the HIRIF for federal administrative expenses to carry out the ACA. [OS]	According to the FY2015 Budget, there was an unobligated balance of $87 million at the beginning of FY2014.

Source: Prepared by the Congressional Research Service based on the text of the Patient Protection and Affordable Care Act (ACA; P.L. 111-148), as amended.

a. Transfers from the two trust funds are in such proportion as the Secretary determines appropriate.

b. Of the amounts appropriated for the period FY2011-FY2019, and for each subsequent 10-year period, at least $25 million must be made available each fiscal year for the selection, testing, and evaluation of new payment and service delivery models.

c. Transfers from the two trust funds are in the same proportion as the Secretary determines under SSA Sec. 1853(f).

d. The health insurance fee is to equal $2 multiplied by the average number of covered lives in a policy/plan year ($1 in the case of a policy/plan year ending during FY2013), updated annually by the rate of medical inflation beginning in FY2015.

e. The trust fund transfers are to equal $2 ($1 in FY2013) multiplied by the average number of individuals entitled to benefits under Part A or enrolled under Part B in a given fiscal year, updated annually by the rate of medical inflation beginning in FY2015.

Table 2. ACA Appropriations and Fund Transfers by Fiscal Year in Which Funds Are Available for Obligation

Dollars in Millions, Includes Funding Extensions and Rescissions

ACA Section	Program	Fiscal Year										Total[a]
		2010	2011	2012	2013	2014	2015	2016	2017	2018	2019	
Private Health Insurance												
1002	Health insurance consumer information	30[b]	(Note: This section also authorizes to be appropriated SSAN for FY2011 and each fiscal year thereafter.)									30
1003	Review of health insurance premium rates	250	—	—	—	—	—	—	—	—	—	250
1101	Temporary high-risk health insurance pools	5,000[b]	—	—	—	—	—	—	—	—	—	5,000
1102	Early retiree reinsurance program	5,000[b]	—	—	—	—	—	—	—	—	—	5,000
1311	Health insurance exchange planning and establishment	Appropriates amounts necessary for grants each fiscal year, as determined by the Secretary; no grant awards after Jan. 1, 2015.										TBD[c]
1322	Consumer operated and oriented plans (CO-OPs)	1,121[d]	—	—	—	—	—	—	—	—	—	1,121[d]
1323	Health insurance exchange subsidies (U.S. territories)	—	—	—	—	$1 billion total for CY2014 through CY2019[e]						1,000
Medicaid and Children's Health Insurance Program (CHIP)												
2701	Medicaid adult health quality measures	60	60	60	60	60	—	—	—	—	—	300[f]
2707	Medicaid emergency psychiatric demonstration	—	75[g]	—	—	—	—	—	—	—	—	75
2801	Medicaid and CHIP Payment and Access Commission	11[h]	(Note: This section also authorizes to be appropriated SSAN for FY2011 and each fiscal year thereafter.)									11
4108	Medicaid prevention and wellness incentives	—	$100 million total for CY2011 through CY2015[f]									100
4306	CHIP childhood obesity demonstration	$25 million total for FY2010 through FY2014					—	—	—	—	—	25
10203(d)	CHIP annual appropriation[i]	—	—	—	—	19,147	21,061	—	—	—	—	40,208
10203(d)	CHIP outreach and enrollment grants	Increases total funding from $100 million to $140 million and extends funding period through FY2015.										40

Fiscal Year

ACA Section	Program	2010	2011	2012	2013	2014	2015	2016	2017	2018	2019	Total[a]
Medicare												
3014	Medicare quality and efficiency measures	20[i]	20	20	20	20	—	—	—	—	—	100
3021(a)	Center for Medicare and Medicaid Innovation	5	$10 billion total for FY2011 through FY2019, and $10 billion for each subsequent 10-year period.									10,005[f]
3024	Medicare independence at home demonstration	5[j]	5	5	5	5	5	—	—	—	—	30
3026	Community-based care transition services	—	$300 million total for FY2011 through FY2015[k]					—	—	—	—	300[k]
3027(b)	Medicare gainsharing demonstration	2	—	—	—	—	—	—	—	—	—	2[f]
3113	Diagnostic laboratory test demonstration	5[l]	—	—	—	—	5	—	—	—	—	5
3306	Outreach and assistance for low-income beneficiaries	$45 million total for FY2010 through FY2012[m]			25[m]	25[m]	12.5[m]	—	—	—	—	107.5
3403	Independent Payment Advisory Board	—	—	5[n]	For FY2013 and each subsequent fiscal year, appropriates previous year's amount adjusted for inflation; funds derived from the Medicare trust funds.[n]							TBD[c]
4202(b)	Prevention and wellness evaluation	50[i]	—	—	—	—	—	—	—	—	—	50
4204(e)	GAO study of Medicare vaccine coverage	1	—	—	—	—	—	—	—	—	—	1
10323(a)	Environmental health pilot program	SSAN[i]	—	—	—	—	—	—	—	—	—	TBD[c]
10323(b)	Environmental health screening and education	$23 million total for FY2010 through FY2014					$20 million total for FY2015 though FY2019, and for each 5-year period thereafter					43[f]
Fraud and Abuse												
6402(i) & HCERA 1303(a)	Health Care Fraud and Abuse Control (HCFAC) Account	—	105	65	40	40	30	30	10	10	10	350[o]
Health Centers												
4101(a)	School-based health center establishment grants	50	50	50	50	—	—	—	—	—	—	200[f]

ACA Section	Program	Fiscal Year										Total[a]
		2010	2011	2012	2013	2014	2015	2016	2017	2018	2019	
10503(b)(1)	Community-based health center operations (CHCF)	—	1,000	1,200	1,500	2,200	3,600	—	—	—	—	9,500[f]
10503(c)	Health center construction and renovation	—	\$1.5 billion total for FY2011 through FY2015					—	—	—	—	1,500[f]
Health Workforce and the National Health Service Corps												
10503(b)(2)	National Health Service Corps (CHCF)	—	290	295	300	305	310	—	—	—	—	1,500[f]
5507(a)	Health workforce demonstration grants	85	85	85	85	85	85[p]	—	—	—	—	510
5507(b)	Family-to-family health information centers	5	5	5	5[q]	5[q]	2.5[q]	—	—	—	—	27.5[f]
5508(c)	Teaching health centers, GME payments	—	SSAN for FY2011 through FY2015, not to exceed \$230 million					—	—	—	—	≤230
5509	Medicare graduate nurse education demonstration	—	—	50	50	50	50	—	—	—	—	200[f]
10502	Health care facility construction	100	—	—	—	—	—	—	—	—	—	100[r]
Community-Based Prevention and Wellness												
4002	Prevention and Public Health Fund	500	750	1,000	1,000	1,000	1,000	1,000	1,000	1,250	1,250	9,750[s]
Maternal and Child Health												
2951	Maternal, infant, and early childhood home visitation	100	250	350	400	400	400[t]	—	—	—	—	1,900
2953	Personal responsibility education program grants	75	75	75	75	75	75[u]	—	—	—	—	450[f]
2954	Abstinence education state grants	50	50	50	50	50	50[v]	—	—	—	—	300
10214	Pregnancy assistance grants	25	25	25	25	25	25	25	25	25	25	250
Long-Term Care												
2403	Medicaid money follows the person demonstration	—	450	450	450	450	450	450	—	—	—	2,700

ACA Section	Program	2010	2011	2012	2013	2014	2015	2016	2017	2018	2019	Total[a]
2405	State Aging and Disability Resource Centers	10	10	10	10	10	—	—	—	—	—	50
6201	Background checks of long-term care providers	Up to $160 million total for FY2010 through FY2012			—	—	—	—	—	—	—	≤160[w]
8002(d)	National Clearinghouse for Long-Term Care Information	—	3	3	0[x]	0[x]	0[x]	—	—	—	—	6
Comparative Effectiveness Research												
6301(d)	Medicare trust fund transfers (PCORTF)	—	—	—	For each of FY2013-FY2019, transfers amounts from the Medicare trust funds as determined by a formula.[y]							TBD[c]
6301(e)	Appropriations and fees (PCORTF)	10	50	150	For each of FY2013-FY2019, appropriates $150 million plus an amount equal to the net revenue from a fee levied on health insurance and self-insured plans.[z]							TBD[c]
Biomedical Research												
9023(e)	Grants for investment in new therapeutics	SSAN	—	—	—	—	—	—	—	—	—	≤1[aa]
ACA Implementation: Administrative Expenses												
HCERA 1005	Health Insurance Reform Implementation Fund	1,000	—	—	—	—	—	—	—	—	—	1,000

Source: Prepared by the Congressional Research Service based on the text of the Patient Protection and Affordable Care Act (ACA; P.L. 111-148), as amended.

Notes: Funds are provided from the Treasury unless otherwise noted. A dash means that ACA does not appropriate or transfer funds for the fiscal year(s) noted.

a. Total represents the cumulative amount of appropriations or fund transfers over the 10-year period FY2010-FY2019. Note that in several instances the 10-year total is yet to be determined (TBD); see table entries for ACA Secs. 1311, 3403, 6301(d) & (e), 9023(e), and 10323(a). In addition, four provisions provide annual or multiple-year appropriations beyond FY2019. The total shown in the table for three of these provisions represents the cumulative amount appropriated through FY2019; see table entries for ACA Secs. 3021(a), 4002 (discussed in table note "s" below), and 10323(b). Finally, the total for ACA Sec. 6402(i) includes an amount appropriated in FY2020 (see table note "o" below).

b. Funds are to remain available without fiscal year limitation.

c. To be determined.

d. ACA Sec. 1322 appropriated $6 billion for the CO-OP program. P.L. 112-10 rescinded $2.2 billion of that amount, and then P.L. 112-74 rescinded an additional $400 million. Finally, P.L. 112-240 rescinded 90% of the program's unobligated balance as of January 2, 2013, and transferred the remaining unobligated funds to a new CO-OP contingency fund to provide assistance and oversight to CO-OP loan recipients. This effectively terminated CMS's authority to make new loan awards. Overall, Congress rescinded a total of $4.879 billion, leaving $1.121 billion of the original $6 billion CO-OP program appropriation.

e. Of this total amount, $925 million is for Puerto Rico, and the remaining $75 million is for the other U.S. territories in amounts as specified by the Secretary.

f. Funds are to remain available until expended.

g. Funds are to remain available for obligation through December 31, 2015.

h. Of this total amount, $9 million is appropriated, and the remaining $2 million is a transfer from CHIP funding for FY2010. Funds are to remain available until expended.

i. Prior to enactment of ACA, the CHIP program was funded through FY2013.

j. The Secretary is required to transfer amounts from the Medicare Part A and Part B trust funds each fiscal year in such proportion as the Secretary determines appropriate. Funds are to remain available until expended.

k. The Secretary is required to transfer amounts from the Medicare Part A and Part B trust funds each fiscal year in such proportion as the Secretary determines appropriate. Funds are to remain available until expended. P.L. 113-6 rescinded $200 million of the ACA's original transfer of $500 million for CCTP.

l. The Secretary is required to transfer the $5 million from the Medicare Part B trust fund, to remain available until expended.

m. The Secretary is required to transfer amounts from the Medicare Part A and Part B trust funds in the same proportion as the Secretary determines under SSA Sec. 1853(f). P.L. 112-240 extended funding for an additional year by transferring $25 million for FY2013 for the four outreach and assistance programs funded by ACA through FY2012. P.L. 113-93 further extended funding for the programs by transferring $25 million for FY2014 and $12.5 million for the first half of FY2015. Funds are to remain available until expended. See **Table 1**.

n. P.L. 112-74 rescinded $10 million of IPAB's $15 million appropriation for FY2012; P.L. 113-6 rescinded $10 million of IPAB's appropriation for FY2013; and P.L. 113-76 rescinded $10 million of IPAB's appropriation for FY2014.

o. Funds are to be appropriated from the Medicare Part A trust fund. Note: the total amount appropriated (i.e., $350 million) includes a final appropriation of $10 million for FY2020.

p. P.L. 113-93 provided an additional year of funding for health workforce demonstration grants.

q. P.L. 112-240 appropriated $5 million for FY2013 for family-to-family health information centers. P.L. 113-67 and P.L. 113-93 provided an additional $5 million for FY2014 and a prorated amount for the first half of FY2015. See **Table 1**.

r. Funds are to remain available for obligation until September 30, 2011.

s. ACA Sec. 4002 originally provided a permanent annual appropriation to the Prevention and Public Health Fund, as follows: FY2010 = $500 million; FY2011 = $750 million; FY2012 = $1 billion; FY2013 = $1.25 billion; FY2014 = $1.5 billion; FY2015 and each year thereafter = $2 billion. P.L. 112-96 reduced the annual appropriations to the PPHF over the period FY2013-FY2021, as follows: FY2013 through FY2017 = $1 billion; FY2018 and FY2019 = $1.25 billion; FY2020 and FY2021 = $1.5 billion; FY2022 and each year thereafter = $2 billion. Thus, appropriations to the fund now total $9.750 billion over the period FY2010-FY2019.

t. P.L. 113-93 appropriated $400 million for the first half of FY2015.

u. P.L. 113-93 provided an additional year of funding for PREP grants.

v. P.L. 113-93 provided an additional year of funding for abstinence education grants.

w. The HHS Secretary is required to notify the Treasury Secretary of the amount necessary to carry out activities under this section for the period of FY2010 through FY2012, but not to exceed $160 million. The Treasury Secretary must then transfer the amount specified from the Treasury to the HHS Secretary. Funds are to remain available until expended.

x. P.L. 112-240 repealed the appropriations for the National Clearinghouse and rescinded all unobligated FY2013 funds (as of January 3, 2013).

y. ACA Sec. 6301(d) provided the following formula for the transfer of funds from the Medicare Part A and Part B trust funds to the PCORTF: (1) for FY2013, an amount from each respective Medicare trust fund equal to $1 multiplied by the average number of individuals entitled to Part A benefits, or enrolled in Part B during that period; and (2) for each of FY2014-FY2019, an amount from each respective Medicare trust fund equal to $2 multiplied by the average number of individuals entitled to Part A benefits, or enrolled in Part B during that fiscal year. Beginning in FY2015, amounts are subject to adjustment for increases in health care spending.

The FY2015 Budget includes the following transfer amounts from the Medicare trust funds to the PCORTF: FY2013 actual = $52 million; FY2014 estimate = $107 million; FY2015 estimate = $117 million.

z. The fee is equal to $2 multiplied by the average number of covered lives in a policy/plan year ($1 in the case of policy/plan years ending during FY2013). Beginning in FY2015, amounts are subject to adjustment for increases in health care spending. The FY2015 Budget includes the following fee revenue: FY2013 actual = $277 million; FY2014 estimate = $347 million; FY2015 estimate = $392 million.

aa. To be determined. ACA Sec. 9023(e) created a two-year tax credit program, subject to an overall cap of $1 billion, for small companies that invest in new therapies to prevent, diagnose and treat cancer and other diseases. The total amount of tax credits any one company can receive for the two years may not exceed $5 million. Companies may elect to receive one or more grants—for which SSAN are appropriated—in lieu of tax credits. Grant applications must be received before January 1, 2013.

Appendix A. Acronyms Used in the Report

The following laws and federal agencies are referred to in this report by their acronym:

ACA	Patient Protection and Affordable Care Act (P.L. 111-148)
ACF	Administration for Children and Families
ACL	Administration for Community Living
AHRQ	Agency for Healthcare Research and Quality
ATRA	American Taxpayer Relief Act of 2012 (P.L. 112-240)
BBEDCA	Balanced Budget and Emergency Deficit Control Act of 1985 (P.L. 99-177)
CBO	Congressional Budget Office
CCIIO	Center for Consumer Information and Insurance Oversight
CDC	Centers for Disease Control and Prevention
CMI	Center for Medicare & Medicaid Innovation
CMS	Centers for Medicare & Medicaid Services
DRA	Deficit Reduction Act of 2005 (P.L. 109-171)
HCERA	Health Care and Education Reconciliation Act of 2010 (P.L. 111-152)
HHS	(Department of) Health and Human Services
HRSA	Health Resources and Services Administration
OS	Office of the Secretary (HHS)
IRC	Internal Revenue Code
IRS	Internal Revenue Service
MIPPA	Medicare Improvements for Patients and Providers Act of 2008 (P.L. 110-275)
OAA	Older Americans Act
OMB	Office of Management and Budget
PAMA	Protecting Access to Medicare Act of 2014 (P.L. 113-93)
PHSA	Public Health Service Act
PSGRRA	Pathway for SGR Reform Act of 2013 (P.L. 113-67, Division B)
SSA	Social Security Act

Appendix B. Annual Spending Reductions Under the Budget Control Act

The Budget Control Act of 2011 (BCA)[19] amended the Balanced Budget and Emergency Deficit Control Act of 1985 (BBEDCA) by establishing two budget enforcement mechanisms to reduce federal spending by at least $2.1 trillion over the 10-year period FY2012 through FY2021. First, the BCA established enforceable limits, or caps, on discretionary spending for each of those years. Second, the BCA created a Joint Committee on Deficit Reduction to develop legislation to further limit federal spending. The failure of the Joint Committee to agree on deficit-reduction legislation triggered automatic annual spending reductions for each of FY2013 through FY2021.

The BCA specified that a total of $109 billion must be cut each year from nonexempt budget accounts. That amount is equally divided between defense and nondefense spending. Within each category—defense and nondefense—the spending cuts are divided proportionately between discretionary spending and nonexempt mandatory (i.e., direct) spending. Under the BCA, the spending reductions are achieved through a combination of sequestration (i.e., an across-the-board cancellation of budgetary resources) and lowering the BCA-imposed discretionary spending caps.

The BCA requires that the mandatory spending reductions in each category—defense and nondefense—must be executed each year by a sequestration of all nonexempt accounts, subject to the BBEDCA sequestration rules. Discretionary spending in each category is also subject to sequestration, but only in FY2013. For each of the remaining fiscal years (i.e., FY2014 through FY2021), discretionary spending reductions are to be achieved by lowering the discretionary spending caps for defense and nondefense spending by the total dollar amount of the reduction. Thus, congressional appropriators get to decide how to apportion the cuts within the lowered spending caps rather than having the cuts applied across-the-board to all nonexempt discretionary spending accounts through sequestration. The Office of Management and Budget (OMB) is responsible for calculating the percentages and amounts by which mandatory and discretionary spending are required to be reduced each year, and for applying the BBEDCA's sequestration exemptions and rules.

The American Taxpayer Relief of 2012 (ATRA)[20] revised the discretionary spending caps for FY2013 and FY2014 and reduced the overall dollar amount that needed to be sequestered from FY2013 defense and nondefense spending. The Bipartisan Budget Act of 2013[21] further revised the spending caps for FY2014 and FY2015 and eliminated the requirements that these caps be lowered pursuant to the BCA's annual spending reductions.[22]

---

[19] P.L. 112-25, 125 Stat. 240.

[20] P.L. 112-240, 126 Stat. 2313.

[21] P.L. 113-67, Division A, 127 Stat. 1165.

[22] For a more complete analysis of the Budget Control Act of 2011 and the amendments that were made to it by the American Taxpayer Relief Act of 2012, see CRS Report R41965, *The Budget Control Act of 2011*, by Bill Heniff Jr., Elizabeth Rybicki, and Shannon M. Mahan; and CRS Report R42949, *The American Taxpayer Relief Act of 2012: Modifications to the Budget Enforcement Procedures in the Budget Control Act*, by Bill Heniff Jr.

Author Contact Information

C. Stephen Redhead
Specialist in Health Policy
credhead@crs.loc.gov, 7-2261

Acknowledgments

The following CRS analysts contributed to earlier versions of this report: Kirsten Colello, Patricia Davis, Gary Guenther, Elayne Heisler, Lisa Herz, Janet Kinzer, Sarah Lister, Alison Mitchell, Bernice Reyes, Amanda Sarata, Carmen Solomon-Fears, Emilie Stoltzfus, and Susan Thaul.

www.ingramcontent.com/pod-product-compliance
Lightning Source LLC
Chambersburg PA
CBHW080749290526

45790CB00008B/3393